ACKNOWLEDGEMENTS

Red Skies	Old weather forecast
Blackbirds	*Tommy Thumb's Pretty Song Book*. 1744
Joseph Addison's Ode	Adapted from his *Ode to Blackbirds*
Little Boy Blue	*The Famous Tommy Thumb's Little Song Book*. 1760
Ballad of Blue China	Andrew Lang (1844-1912)
Fog, Filthy Air & Graymalkin	From *Macbeth* by William Shakespeare
Green Gown	*Songs for the Nursery*. 1805
Green Peace	Adapted from a passage in *The Silent Echo* by Bruce McNally
Vinegar & Brown Paper	*Mother Goose's Melodies*, 1765
Mulberry Bush	Old nursery song
Lilac Time	From *Barrel Organ* by Alfred Noyes (1880-1958)

THE ZEBRA

The zebra's neither black nor white
But has acquired the knack
Of being black AND being white
Or is it white and black?

Text copyright © 1992 by Hiawyn Oram. Illustrations copyright © 1992 by David McKee.

The rights of Hiawyn Oram and David McKee to be identified as the author and illustrator of this work have been asserted by them in accordance with the Copyright, Designs and Patents Act, 1988.

First published in Great Britain in 1992 by Andersen Press Ltd., 20 Vauxhall Bridge Road, London SW1V 2SA. Published in Australia by Random Century Australia Pty., Ltd., 20 Alfred Street, Milsons Point, Sydney, NSW 2061. All rights reserved. Colour separated and printed in Italy.

British Library Cataloguing in Publication Data available.

ISBN 0-86264-384-8

1   2   3   4   5   6   7   8   9   10

OUT OF THE BLUE

STORIES AND POEMS ABOUT COLOUR

WRITTEN BY HIAWYN ORAM
ILLUSTRATED BY DAVID McKEE

Andersen Press · London

RED RAG TO LITTLE BULL

Little Bull lived with his mother in a field. One day he found her crying. "It is bad news," she wept. "I have just heard your father is dead. And soon they will come for you and you will be dead too."

Now Little Bull was very fond of being alive and insisted she explain. So Little Bull's mother told him of the bullfights in the city and of the bullfighters who would taunt him with red rags until he went wild and charged.

"But charging doesn't make me dead," said Little Bull.

"No," said his mother, "but once you charge, even though they have made you do it, they will kill you in the name of self-defence."

Little Bull was deeply shocked. "In that case when the bullfighters wave their red rags I will not charge. I will ignore them."

"It is not that easy," said his mother. "You have never seen red and so you do not know what it will do to you. You will charge. That is what bulls do when they see red. You will not be able to help yourself."

At this Little Bull's heart sank. But he did not give up hope and when they came to take him to the bullrings he comforted his mother. "Save your tears. I'll be back."

And a few weeks later he was.

"Little Bull!" cried his mother, "How did you do it?"

"How do you think?" said Little Bull.

"I do not know. It is a miracle. Tell me!"

"I closed my eyes," said Little Bull. "And I would not open them."

"You mean you have been into the bullrings of the big city and you haven't yet seen red?" cried his mother.

"No," said Little Bull, "I haven't, and now I don't intend to."

But he did. That summer, like hundreds of red rags to Little Bull, the poppies grew in the field. And it is true to say, they had a terrible time of it.

RED SKIES

Red sky at night
Is a shepherd's delight
Red sky in the morning
Is a shepherd's warning

TWO REDHEADS ARE BETTER THAN ONE

Rachel the Redhead was all in despair
  Hating the sight of her head of red hair
She lived in the bathroom but couldn't repair
  Not the flaming red red of THAT head of red hair

Then along came a knight in some armour all shining
  Who said to her, "Rachel, now why are you whining?
I've searched the whole earth for a head to compare
  With the flaming red red of MY head of red hair."

Then he took off his helmet, how Rachel did stare
  Seeing the sight of his head of red hair
And soon they were married and loving the glare
  Of the flaming red red of TWO heads of red hair

RED BERRIES

Red can warn but red can also attract . . . Birds cannot resist red berries, which is exactly what nature intended . . . for the berries only turn red when the seeds are ready for sowing . . . by the very birds that cannot resist them . . .

RED TAPE

A stickler from down in the Cape
Liked everything tied in red tape
But what a to do
When he found he was too
And no one would help him escape

THE CARDINAL'S HAT

Once there was a cardinal who was always sad for he never felt he was quite close enough to God.

One day he was standing on his balcony staring longingly up at the heavens when a bird flew down onto the railing.

"Why so sad, Cardinal?" said the bird.

"Oh, I don't know," sighed the cardinal. "I love God so much and I'm sure he doesn't realise it."

"Then you must fly up there and tell Him at once," said the bird.

"But how?" said the cardinal. "I have no wings."

"I shall be your messenger," said the bird. "I will go for you. But first you must give me your red cardinal's hat or I will never get an audience."

So the cardinal put his red hat on the bird's head. The bird flew away with it, laughing all the way to the woods, and has been called a Cardinal Bird ever since.

RED HERRING

There was a pack of fox hounds being trained to follow a trail. The trainer got some herrings that had been smoked until they were red. He rubbed them under the noses of the hounds, dragged them through the bushes and fields and sent the hounds haring after their scent.

But one of the hounds was cleverer than the rest.

"Bah," he said, "how stupid does that trainer think we are? That's not a fox he's set us after, that's a red herring," and he disappeared in disgust to find the real thing.

And the hound's intelligence must have started something because to this day, anything waved in front of somebody's nose to seem like the real thing is called a red herring.

RED BREAST

Said Swallow to the Robin, "It really gets me down
That you have such a red breast while mine is mainly brown"
Said Robin, "You migrate, sir, and so you do not know
A robin's breast is red, sir, to brighten up the snow."

RED GIANTS AND RED DWARVES

The stars are suns, giants and dwarves, all of different size, brightness, colour and temperature. The hottest stars in the universe are the youngest, where temperatures reach 80,000°C. They're so hot they're white. The older and more developed stars get, the cooler and redder they become.

Well-known reds are *Betelgeux* and *Antares*, both supergiants at around 3,000°C. *Proxima Centauri* is a red dwarf at a mild 3,400°C and *R. Leporis* is one of the coolest red dwarves at 2,500°C.

Our sun, which people sometimes call the *Red Giant*, isn't. It's a yellow dwarf baking away at a pleasant 5,000°C.

SONG OF THE CARNIVORE

Oh, I do like lobster, sang the Carnivore
And I will wear cherry which I quite adore
And I have a pair of shoes in the vein of cheese
And a hat in the colour of strawberries
And I will say currant's very bright and bold
While a flame-red chilli doesn't leave me cold
But talk of a red good enough to eat
And there's NOTHING like the BLOOD-RED RED OF MEAT!

EMBARRASSMENT

You might wish it was white, you might wish it was blue
You might wish that it never would happen to you
But scarlet, tomato, crimson or rose
Is the way that it happens, the way that it goes
When you're put on the spot or they call out your name
Or your mother is making you curl up with shame
You can feel it all fiery and rising apace
Right up from your shoecaps full speed to your face
You can wish it was primrose or deep bottle green
Or something less glaring and easily seen
But there is no escaping, it has to be said
– Embarrassment ALWAYS comes in red

SUNNY REFLECTIONS

Without the sun we wouldn't have life
  We wouldn't have wheat, we wouldn't have corn
Without the sun we wouldn't have known
  We didn't have life – we wouldn't be born

RIPE CORN

Her hair was the colour of ripened corn
A colour, she thought, she couldn't adorn
'Till binding it up with cornflowers blue
The mouse said "Cor!" and the cows said
  "Moo"
And the farmer's son said, "I love you!"

DANDELION

The dandelion though but a weed
Like golden cheer does grow
And when its flower has turned to puff
It kindly lets us know
"He loves me, he loves me not, he loves me, I
  KNEW IT!
He loves me, he loves me not – Oh,
  Dandelion, YOU BLEW IT!"

STRAW'S GOLD

Though straw looks gold, to most of us
It is a simple thing
To those with wintering cows to feed
Straw is king.

THE SUNFLOWER AND THE CROCUS

Said the Sunflower to the Crocus,
"For man's nutritional needs
I'm most important, I give my seeds."

Said the Crocus to the Sunflower
Your seeds are good of course,
But I give them saffron, I flavour sauce."

YELLOW DOG, RUNNING

The dog was a mongrel, from a long line of mongrels, outcasts, bin-dogs and scavengers. His mangy short-haired coat was of such a dirty gamboge yellow no eye ever warmed to him and no one wanted him about the house. His body, like a badly made sausage, was perched on top of legs so long and thin the whole defied any sense of grace or proportion. And if that wasn't enough, from accident or birth, one of his back legs was crippled. This gave his running action such an unnatural and desperate air that the local children became thoroughly over-excited by it. Soon throwing stones so they could "Watch Yellow Dog run," became their most popular pastime.

And then something eerie occurred. The boy who had always led the stone-throwing fell on hard times. He started going round in rags, never washed and gradually turned a gamboge colour himself. He took to scavenging and stealing until one day, running away with a purse, he got knocked down and one of his legs was crippled. Soon the local children noticed how desperate he looked when he ran and after that when the cruel cry went up after school, "C'mon, let's make Yellow Dog run!" the answering cry usually was, "Which one?"

SCARED YELLOW

There once was a cowardly fellow
Who wobbled, when challenged, like jello
Though his hair hadn't greyed
From being afraid
His skin had gone cadmium yellow

THE PRIMROSE PATH

I took the primrose path through woods
When I was six or seven
And thought I must have stumbled on
The scenic route to heaven

SONG OF THE LEMON

Sour as puss, and bitter maybe
*   But think of me sliced in hot black tea*
And what of the scent of Lemon Verbena
*   When added to soap – you'll never feel cleaner*
And who put the lemon in lemon meringue
*   Or gave bags of sherbet their twist and their tang*
And some time ago when sailors grew nervy
*   And crabby and scabby, I cured them of scurvy*
So no matter how bitter my rind or my juices
*   The song that I sing is – a lemon has uses*

VARIATIONS ON A YELLOW THEME

In London
Cowardy cowardy custard,
Can't eat bread and mustard

In Glasgow
Cowardy cowardy custard
Three bags of mustard
One for you
And one for me
And one for cowardy custard

In Preston
Cowardy cowardy custard
Your bones will turn to mustard

In Pendeen
Cowardy cowardy custard
Dip your head in granny's mustard

In Lydney
Cowardy cowardy custard
Fell in his mother's mustard
The mustard was hot
He swallowed the lot
Cowardy cowardy custard

In Oxford
Eggy! Yolky!

YELLOW WITH AGE

It is said things mellow with age, which often means they yellow with age. To test the truth of that, look at any old book or photograph or collection of newspaper cuttings, or watch the leaves in autumn.

Yellowing usually has to do with long exposure to the chemicals in air. Slowly, invisibly at first, these react with other chemicals – in paper, wood, paint canvas, linen or even skin – and gradually the colour-change occurs. With leaves, however, it has more to do with sap drying up as summer and the growing season comes to an end.

YELLOW SOAP

*To make a bar of yellow soap
And wash yourself of odour
Mix some tallow with some rosin
And a spoon of soda*

NIGHT

Black as night, they say, for black is night
* The velvet of her cloak absorbs all light*
She gives no quarter and she asks for none
* And neither pines nor hankers for the missing sun*
Black as jet, she strides, black pearl is night
* Who gives her loyal subjects undimmed sight*
The owl, the bat, the sweet-songed nightingale
* To all who live and walk with her she lifts her veil*
Till they become the jewels that glitter in her crown
* And wish their Queen's ascendance and the sun forever down*

MOURNING DRESS

They all wore black to Granpa's funeral
* It seemed a way to say*
"The colour that you brought our lives
* Has dimmed and gone away"*
Then, in a week, to our surprise
* Gran started wearing red*
But she explained "I'll live for two
* Now one of us is dead"*

LIQUORICE STICKS

Some say "comforters" and some say "chews"
* And some say "lollies-on-sticks"*
But I say "Half-a-pound-of-allsorts-please
* An'-sixteen-stickerish-licks"*

THE BLACK HOLE

Somewhere in the galaxy it happened
A massive star collapsed like shattered glass
Till gravitation pulled the bits together
So densely not a ray of light could pass
Then round itself – this tightly shrunken
  matter
This dark and suicidal shrunken shape –
It gathered a protectorate, it colonised the
  space
Making sure from this protectorate not a thing
  could now escape . . .
Then a chorus of the mothers of young
  meteors and 'ites
The planets and the comets and the smaller
  cluster lights
Rose like any chorusing of frightened mothers
  might
DON'T GO NEAR THE BLACK HOLE,
DON'T GO NEAR THE BLACK HOLE
DON'T GO NEAR THE BLACK HOLE,
  LITTLE DARLINGS, TONIGHT!

THE CROW, THE RAVEN AND THE ROOK

The Crow, the Raven and the Rook
  All met to have a jaw
'Bout history and politics
  And why they weren't loathed more
"I cheat, I swindle and I thieve
  I have a raucous caw"
Declared the Rook. "I'm quite perplexed
  That I'm not loathed much more."
"I feed on carrion and on flesh
  The rotting I adore"
The Raven said. "I'm quite perplexed
  That I'm not loathed much more."
"I go unchecked, I steal their grain
  I eat their chickens raw"
Announced the Crow, "I'm most surprised
  We're ALL not loathed much more –
Yet feel that for the reason
  We needn't search too far
It's simply that they understand
  What characters we are"

JOSEPH ADDISON'S ODE

Blackbirds in the garden
Eating up the cherries
Frankly for their cheerful songs
I'd give them all the berries

THE BLACK PATCH

My Uncle wears a black patch when he comes
  to us for tea
And he says he was a pirate which I'm sure he
  says for me
'Cos though he knows of pirate gold he'll dig
  up one dark night –
SOME days it's his left eye that he patches –
  some the right

BLACK BOOK

"You're going down in my Black Book
   You haven't passed the test"
The King cried to his Admiralty
   "Your crimes you've not confessed"
"Oh please not that, Your Majesty
   Not down with all the rest"
The Admiral wept upon his knees
   "We did our level best"
"Then best just wasn't good enough
   I'll hear no more of it
You've fallen out of favour"
   Yelled the King, "AND IT IS WRIT!"

BLACKBIRDS

Sing a song of sixpence
   A pocket full of rye
Four and twenty blackbirds
   Baked in a pie
When the pie was opened
   The birds began to sing
Wasn't that a dainty dish
   To set before a king?

The king was in his counting house
   Counting out his money
The Queen was in her parlour
   Eating bread and honey
The maid was in the garden
   Hanging out the clothes
When down flew a blackbird
   And pecked off her nose

LITTLE BOY BLUE

Little Boy Blue, come blow your horn
  The sheep's in the meadow, the cow's in the corn
Where is the boy who looks after the sheep?
  He's under the haystack fast asleep
Will you awake him? No, not I
  For if I do he will only cry

THE BUSHMAN'S BLUEY

Over his shoulder the Bushman slings
  All that he owns, important things
A can for his billy, a hunting knife
  And p'rhaps if he had one, one good wife
And he bundles them up in a blanket of blue
  And wherever he goes, that Bluey goes too

OUT OF THE BLUE

Out of the blue, into the blue
The meteor span and span
Towards the blue of infinity
From the blue where it all began

BLUE-EYED BOY
A Confusing Story

Our brother Jack was favourite
Ma bought him every toy
She used to stroke his hair and say
"And how's my blue-eyed boy?"
Well, we could hardly bear that
It made us feel so down
For Jess and I had blue eyes
And Jack's were walnut brown.

BLUE BLOOD

When we're cold our hands go blue
  As if our blood had gone blue too
Just like they say of Queens and Kings
  And Duchesses and Counts and things
Which seems to show quite possibly
  To some extent or small degree
We're all quite royal and not been told
  And only show it when we're cold.

THE BALLAD OF BLUE-STOCKING BELLA

Blue-Stocking Bella was clever as clever
  Blue-Stocking Bel was a swat
Her head she kept down
  In her books with a frown
She was crazy to know what was what

Blue-Stocking Bella was clever as clever
  Blue-Stocking Bel was a brain
When teased and called "Smarty"
  She took up karate
And never got laughed at again

NEVERNESS

Once in a blue moon, they say
Once in a blue moon
But as the moon is never blue
You know it won't be soon

BALLAD OF BLUE CHINA

There's a joy without canker or cark
There's a pleasure eternally new
'Tis to gloat on the glaze and the mark
Of china that's ancient and blue

FORGET-ME-KNOTS

Forget-Me-Not, Forget-Me-Not
Though your flower is small
Forget me not, Forget-me-Nots
And I'll remember all

THE BLUES

A bluebottle's blue
  And a bluebell's blue
And so is a cloudless sky
  And the eggs of a coot
And a sailor's suit
  And a helping of blueberry pie

An eye can be blue
  And a bruise can be too
But surely no blue can compare
  To the one that is found
When we're flailing around
  In the bottomless depths of despair

CARPET OF BLUE

It can happen, it can happen
Late in April, early May
You don't think you'll come across it
So it takes your breath away
You'll have entered on the hillside
Through the fence you always use
To the woods you always walk in
Round the way you always choose
When you stumble on the bluebells
And it seems a fact to you
That there's never been a carpet
Quite so beautiful or blue

BLUE JEANS

Now, everyone has at least one favourite pair
For days when the question is "What shall I wear?"
But Barnaby Brown, though we tease him and scoff
He lives in his favourites and won't take them off
He wears them at weekends, he wears them to school
He wears them to bed and to bath, as a rule
His mother now says (though she used to make scenes)
That Barnaby thinks he was BORN in blue jeans

THE DEVIL AND THE DEEP BLUE SEA

The fisherboy had strayed where he had been forbidden to go: onto the long thin skerry that ran out like a tongue of rocks into the sea. But his catch had been poor all day and it was well known that the lobsters off the skerry were huge and so he decided to risk his father's wrath should he be found out. Whistling, the boy now clambered to the end of the skerry and dropped his baited lobster pots into the churning waters below. It was only after he could see two fat lobsters in each pot and was hauling them back up that he heard the laugh and felt the gaze on his neck, like two clammy hands.

He spun round and in his fright let go of the ropes so that the pots fell back into the sea and were swept away. But the loss of a fine catch and two good pots meant nothing to the boy now. Coming towards him was the very devil, Old Hornie himself, complete with goat-nimble hooves and a pair of blue horns, like sirens, protruding from his hairless head.

"Yes?" the fisherboy said sharply as if to hold off the devil's advance. "What d'you want on skerry?"

"You," said the devil, coming so close the boy could feel his breath as wet as sea spray. "You, an honest fisherboy who takes nothing from no one but the sea when she affords it and who puts back his tiddlers. Quite a catch for Old Diabolus, huh?" The devil laughed again and raised his clammy blueish hands as if to bring them down like meat hooks onto the boy's shoulders. The boy looked desperately round for an escape, but the devil blocked the way down the skerry to the mainland and behind him crashed the deep blue sea. He hesitated, unable to choose between these two ends, death by drowning seeming as diabolical as falling into the devil's clutches.

Then something caught his eye. A small yellow boat had been thrown by the tide into the waves below him. Now he didn't hesitate but jumped and, managing to land without upsetting the little craft, rowed as hard as he could to safety. And never wishing to be caught between the devil and the deep blue sea again, the boy avoided the skerry for the rest of his fishing days, no matter how tempting the size of the lobsters.

WEARING THE PINK

A fox-hunter's coat is scarlet, but it is always called pink, even to the point where sometimes fox-hunters themselves are called 'pinks'. This tradition goes back so far nobody knows how it began. Perhaps the first fox-hunters were colour-blind or perhaps they were just perverse.

LITTLE PINK PIGS

Little pink pigs with your curly tails
No wonder the noise you're makin'
For today you're the farmyard darlin' dears
And tomorrow you're ham and bacon!

CORAL TROUT

Down in the ocean the Coral Trout is swimming
The Coral Trout is grazing but she doesn't come to grief
For down in the ocean the Coral Trout looks coral
And predators can't tell her from a coral Coral Reef

SHOCKING PINK

Shocking pink is shocking
And it never shows restraint
And in garters round a stocking
It can cause strong men to faint

PINK BLANCMANGE

Wibbly wobbly pink blancmange
Served with lumpy custard
I would rather eat my shoe
Served with English mustard

NEWBORN PINK

Pink from your top
  Pink to your toes
Wrapped in warm blankets
  And soft baby clothes
That you're so newborn
  Quite clearly shows
In the pink from your top
  To your little pink toes

IN THE PINK

To be in the pink is to be in the prime
  And the peak of a perfect condition
With each muscle so fit you'll be entering it
  In a Picture-of-Health competition
To be in the pink is to feel like a cloud
  Of pinks – and as fit as a fiddle
With a fresh glowing skin you're quite comfortable in –
  And NO saggy bits in the middle

SMOKE

The grey smoke rising from the valley
    In a thin but strong and steady winding line
When you're trudging through a cold and rainy evening
    Somehow comes as such a very welcome sign
For if there's smoke, then somewhere in the valley,
    A fire must burn that gives a warming glow
A kettle's on the boil, people live there that's for sure
    Which is always very comforting to know

ROOFTOPS IN THE RAIN

On any dry and cloudless day
It's true to say that slate looks grey
But when the rooves are wet with rain
Before you say it, look again

DAPPLE-GREY

I took my horse to market
And lost her on the way
For dappled were the moors with rain
And she was dapple-grey

FOG, FILTHY AIR & GRAYMALKIN

First Witch
When shall we three meet again?
In thunder, lightning, or in rain?
Second Witch
When the hurlyburly's done
When the battle's lost and won.
Third Witch
That will be ere the set of sun.
First Witch
Where the place?
Second Witch
Upon the heath.
Third Witch
There to meet with Macbeth.

(a cat miaows from off)

First Witch
I come, Graymalkin!

(a toad croaks from off)

Second Witch
Paddock calls.
Third Witch
Anon!
All Three Witches
Fair is foul, and foul is fair:
Hover through the fog and filthy air.

THE GREY FRIAR

A Friar from Grey Friar's Friary
Was found with a blasphemous diary
It said, "Oh dear God
Please don't find this odd
But I long for a habit more fiery"

GREY WOLF

Why do you howl so, Great Grey Wolf
And silence sabotage
Is it because the Moon's so bright
It spoils your camouflage?

GREY HEADS

Is it with too much worrying
That grown-ups' heads go grey
From endless making unmade beds
And slaving hard all day?
Is it from too much stress and strife
And not going out to play?
Or all their wayward children
Who have made them go that way?
Well, maybe grey is hurried on
By these and other scenes
But mostly there's no helping it
It's programmed in the genes

GREY DOVE AND THE GREYBEARD

Old Greybeard had a grey beard
  And sat upon the wall
And sat there quite unhearing
  Till came the Grey Dove's call
"Oh, Greybeard, lend me nesting
  Inside your stately beard
Then I shall pass unnoticed
  And all my brood be reared."

SONG OF THE GREY SUITS

Grey, grey, grey
  Day after day after day
If you want to do well in the Dull Brigade
  You mustn't be seen in another shade
But grey, grey, grey

Grey, grey, grey
  Day after day after day
When a man pinned a rose to his grey lapel
  He was lost to the ranks and condemned to hell
For stepping from line and for getting away
  From grey, grey, GREY!

MARMALADE

Thick cut, thin cut, we all know the drill
From oranges from Africa, more usually
    Seville
Bittersweet like everything the British treasure
    most
Breakfast ISN'T British without marmalade on
    toast!

SUCK AN ORANGE

Suck an orange till it's dry
Quench a burning need
But just in case tomorrow's hot
Also plant the seed

ORANGE COUNTRY

Wherever the sun beats long and hard for
  hours in the sky
And people long for evening and a breeze to
  hover by
Wherever the bay and laurel beat the dust and
  drought and grow
There you'll find the orange tree – aglow

THE MARIGOLD AND THE SUN

When the sun is in the sky
When the sun's out so am I
But when the sun is indisposed
Don't expect much – I'll be closed

SORRY, GOLDFISH

China bred you, China brought you
  To the ornamental pond
Where your gleaming fin gave glimpses
  Of exotic worlds beyond
China bred you, China brought you
  To the common household bowl
Where the ginger tabby waited –
  Thought you lunch and ate you whole

A RECIPE FOR ORANGEADE

INGREDIENTS
The juice of four juicy oranges
The juice of two juicy lemons
The grated rind of four oranges
The grated rind of one lemon
450g white sugar
1.65 litres cold water

METHOD
Wash and grate the rind of the oranges and lemon. Put grated rind aside. Cut, squeeze and strain the juice from the fruit. Melt the sugar in the water over a low heat until you have a smooth syrup. Bring to simmering point but do not boil. Remove from heat. Add the fruit juices and the grated rind. Stir well and leave to cool for 3 hours then refrigerate. Serve chilled with soda water and ice. Keep refrigerated – use within two or three days.

BRASSY LASS

There once was a lass from Likasi
Who thought herself frightfully classy
Then she broke all the rules
By wearing cheap jewels
And ended up feeling quite brassy

PHINONYCTERIS AURANTIA, THE BAT

Phinonycteris Aurantia, the Bat
  Wears a furry orange robe without a hat
And he's found in this regalia
  Round the graves of North Australia
Where you're welcome to pop up and have a chat

Phinonycteris Aurantia, the Bat
  Is as orange as an orange – fancy that
So unlike his fellow flyers
  Who steal black-as-night right by us
You can always see which cemet'ry he's at

DOWN IN THE ORANGERY, NOW

Once in the Hot House orange trees bloomed
  And lovers went down there to kiss
But if you go down to the Orangery now
  There's something you'll probably miss
For though there are orange trees tended and groomed
  And benches for lovers to boot
There's no heady scent, for the flowers and leaves
  Are plastic – and so is the fruit

WHITEWASH

Mrs Hickory's house was in a terrible state of disrepair. Birds, bats and hornets had found nesting in its crumbling crevices. Shutters and sills flaked away. Woodworm was in the doors and the once neat picket fence. At last Mrs Hickory called in the decorators, Bodgit and Scarper. "Do not worry, Mrs Hickory," said Mr Bodgit, "we'll put this mess right in no time." "No time," said Mr Scarper. "Thank you," said Mrs Hickory, and went inside to make tea.

Bodgit and Scarper took out their buckets, threw in lime, added water and – a big brush in each hand – began to slap the mixture all over the house, slap, slap, slap.

When Mrs Hickory came out she clapped her hands. Her house, so recently in disrepair, looked gleaming white and new. "How did you do it?" she cried.

"We whitewashed it," said Mr Bodgit and, taking all the money Mrs Hickory had, they scarpered. And in no time at all the house returned to a state of disrepair for whitewash only ever covers the cracks. It doesn't fix them.

THE LILY

They cast her in plaster and alabaster
  And only felt silly
For nothing could capture her likeness or whiteness
  Nothing could capture the lily

SNOW

It fell while we were sleeping
I think it fell all night
It fell just like a blanket
    And wrapped the world in white
It took away the edges
    And levelled high and low
And made the shortest distance
    An eternity of snow

THE POLAR BEAR

Look, look, there's a polar bear
    Where? Where? I see no bear
There! There! Turned to go
    White as ice! On the floe
No! No! There's no bear
    Here, there or anywhere
No bear at all, what is the fuss –
    Well, only this: HE'S NOW SEEN US

BE GONE, JACK FROST

Jack Frost is a-creeping out across the lands
With icicles for fingers he's working with both hands
And where he breathes his breathing is icing up the fen
    – Be gone, Jack Frost, and never come here again

CLEAN WHITE SHEETS

Clean white sheets, when the washing's done
  Blowing in the breeze, soaking up the sun
Clean white sheets, once the corners meet
  Ironed smooth and flat, smelling fresh and sweet
Clean white sheets, now I'm counting sheep
  There isn't any other place I'd rather fall asleep

THE WHITER TOOTH FAIRY

We've a very fussy fairy who drops in sometimes
  at night
And she leaves us one pound fifty if the tooth is
  very white
But for yellow ones or grey ones or for filled ones
  or for brown
She will only leave us five pence which is very
  putting down
So there's William and there's Christopher, (my
  brothers,) and there's me
And we're brushing in the bathroom, how we're
  brushing, boy, are we
'Cos from now on when we leave our fairy
  gnashers in the night
We are not accepting five pence so we've got to get
  them white!

WHITE ELEPHANTS

The good women of the town were arranging the church bazaar. They had organised Mrs Brown to sell cakes and Mrs Green to sell jumble. Mrs Black had persuaded her husband to do conjuring tricks and Mrs Garnet had agreed to do the teas. Only Mrs Grey had no part to play.

"There must be something you can think of to sell for us," said the vicar's wife.

"My white elephants," said Mrs Grey.

"White elephants!" said the vicar's wife. "There are no such things!"

"I have two," said Mrs Grey. "They were wedding presents and have always been quite useless. Why, they don't even have slots in their backs to act as money boxes!"

"And I have a sombrero given me by a travelling cousin," said Mrs Green, "and as I shan't be going to Mexico in this lifetime, you could sell that!"

"And come to think of it, I have a cocktail shaker I'd be only too glad to get rid of," said Mrs Brown, "for mine is a teetotal household!"

Then all the women remembered things they had, as good as new, for which they had no use or purpose but someone else might. And they all agreed to bring them to the church hall on the day of the bazaar so Mrs Grey could sell them.

"We shall call it the White Elephant Stall," said the vicar's wife jubilantly, "after Mrs Grey's white elephants, and if it is a success we shall have one every year." And it was and they did.

GREEN BEHIND THE EARS

If you are called a greenhorn
  Or green behind the ears
Take no offence (though some is meant
  By those of many years)
For all it says in its mild way
  Is this: Your spring's just sprung
Your life is new and it's quite clear
  That you are very young

GREEN FINGERS

Mrs McGinty had fingers of green
  It wasn't believed until it was seen
What Mrs McGinty could grow, I mean
  'Tatoes, tomatoes, cauli and bean
Carrot and broc'li with turnip between
  Geraniums pink and geraniums red
Orchids exotic and none of them dead
  Profusions of fuschias and roses in tubs
Flowering cherries and flowering shrubs
And all from the having of fingers so green
  And all in an ordin'ry soup tureen

TEN GREEN BOTTLES

Ten green bottles hanging on the wall
  If one green bottle should accidentally fall
There'll be nine green bottles hanging from the wall

Nine green bottles hanging on the wall
  If one green bottle should accidentally fall
There'll be eight green bottles hanging from the wall

Eight, seven, six, five, four, three, two . . .

One green bottle hanging on the wall
  If one green bottle should accidentally fall
There'll be NO green bottles hanging from the wall

GREEN CHEESE

The moon is made from green cheese
For centuries people cried
Till Armstrong, Aldrin and Collins
Discovered they had lied

GREEN PEACE

I'd leave the road on summer days
    Along the path I knew
Beside the clear and babbling stream
    Where Lady's Slippers grew
And find my place inside the wood
    Where insects twinkled gold
And warblers fussed in emerald trees
    Dependable and old
And there I'd sit, alone and still
    And breathe the green like air
Until my old friend, Peace, arrived
    – We always met in there

THE GREEN-EYED MONSTER

Jealousy's a monster and its eyes are slimy green
    And it has a slimy look upon its face
And once it's up and running, using wicked guile and cunning,
    It will nobble any rival in the race

Yes, Jealousy's a monster though it's hardly ever seen
    For it slithers in before we know it's there
But once behind our feelings it will orchestrate our dealings
    Making US the green-eyed monsters – So BEWARE!

QUITE GREEN WITH IT

Ellie was sick, Ellie was ailing
  Her skin was as green as a leaf
A doctor was called, two nurses installed
  Her mother was crying with grief
"Oh, what is the matter, dear doctor, dear man
  Diagnose it as quick as quick as you can
Has she eaten too much or something that's bad
  Or was it those trifles I know that she had
For though she's no glutton and only gets thinner
  She does like her puddings and does like her dinner . . ."

Now the doctor was good, as good as you'll get
  As good as a mother could find
But though he was called and nurses installed
  They couldn't read Eleanor's mind
For the matter, in fact, with young Ellie that night
  Was nothing to do with her diet, poor mite,
But simply a terrible vivid-green dose
  Of a thing that is caught from being too close
To those who have everything when you have not
  Called Wanting-What-Everyone-Else-Has-Got

THE GREEN LIGHT

If it's red,
STOP
If it's yellow
PAUSE
If it's green
GO AHEAD
The world is yours

GREENS, GREENS, EAT YOUR GREENS

Greens, greens, eat your greens
  Put some on your knife
For greens are full of living things
  Greens are full of life

Greens, greens, eat your greens
  Every time you're fed
Then you'll be full of living things
  A living thing, not dead

GREENER GRASS

Once there were two sheep who lived in a luscious green field with a fine flock, a fine shepherd and a fine sheepdog. But they were not content.

"Will you look at the grass in the next field?" said the first.

"It's greener," said the second.

"And the flock, the shepherd and the sheepdog are finer," said the first.

"Then we should go there at once," said the second.

So they chewed their way through the hedgerow and went into the next field.

To their surprise when they got there the grass wasn't any greener and the flock, the shepherd and the sheepdog weren't any finer than in their own field.

"Never mind," said the first sheep, "look at the field next to this. The grass is certainly greener there!"

"And the flock and the shepherd and the sheepdog finer," said the second.

So they chewed their way through the hedgerow surrounding the second field and went into the third.

But, to their amazement, when they got *there*, the grass wasn't any greener and the flock, the shepherd and the sheepdog weren't any finer than in either the first or second field.

"Look," said the second sheep, "at this rate we might just as well go back to the first field where we belong."

"You can," said the first sheep, "but I'm not, for I've been looking at the grass in the *next* field and anyone can see it is definitely greener and the flock, the shepherd and the sheepdog definitely finer."

So the second sheep went back to the first field alone and lived there contentedly while the first sheep went on from field to field always thinking that the grass would be greener and the flock, the shepherd and the sheepdog would be finer. And they never were, but he never learned.

GREEN GOWN

Daffy-down dilly is new come to town
In a yellow petticoat and a green gown

BROWN OWL

Brown Owl sits and stares and winks
  And looks as though she wisely thinks
And knows the spirit, essence, sum
  Of all on life's curriculum
Yet I bet we'd prob'ly find
  If we could read the Brown Owl's mind
Of mysteries and hidden meanings
  Sciences and sudden gleanings
Languages and complex words
  She knows no more than other birds
But if I'm wrong and she's the goods
  The Albert Einstein of the woods
It surely comes as no surprise
  'Twas listening that made her wise

THE NUT-BROWNS

Almonds, walnuts, hazels, cob
  Chestnuts roasted on the hob
Cashews, filberts and there's still
  Pine-nuts, pecans and Brazil
Yet how this nut-brown rhyme deceives
  For it's describing autumn leaves

BROWNIES

Brownies, as everyone knows, are household hobgoblins – small, rough and hairy with an earthy brown skin, to be found all over the lowlands of Scotland, the north and east of England and the Midlands. They will work for nothing, all around the house, scrubbing baths and putting out the garbage, so long as they're left a little good food in return.

But they're tricky characters and if you put a foot wrong in your dealings with them they will leave you immediately. For example, they do not like any attention drawn to gifts for they hate to be expected to show gratitude as much as they hate to be shown it. So when you leave food out for brownies you should do it in such a way that it seems they've found it for themselves. This way the whole "You-did-this-for-me-so-I'm-giving-this-to-you" business is avoided.

Another difficulty with brownies is clothes. Brownies adore clothes, but the minute they're left any they disappear. No one knows if all that happens is that they run back to Hobgoblin County (or wherever it is they live) to show off the clothes or whether they disappear so they don't have to say thank you.

Most important of all, if you do give your brownie a gift of clothes, make sure they're of the best quality or he'll not only leave you but curse you and the smooth running of your household as well.

BROWN PAPER

Brown paper's thick and brown paper's strong
And brown paper's useful 'cos it lasts so long
And brown paper's best when you've got some string
And you're wrapping up any sort of funny-shaped thing

BROWN BEAR

My North American Grizzly Bear
  When he's not skulking in his lair
May well be fishing by the lake
  Or searching out a honey cake

My North American Grizzly Bear
  When he's not here, he's always there
Or sharpening up his yellow claws
  Or pushing open cabin doors

My North American Grizzly Bear
  Is not the sort to call "My dear"
Unless of course it's time for bed
  When he returns to being Ted

HOT COMFORT

In all the world, of anything
Of all the drinks most comforting
There's none I'd like to nominate
As warming-up hot choc-o-late

VINEGAR & BROWN PAPER

Jack and Jill went up the hill
  To fetch a pail of water
Jack fell down and broke his crown
  And Jill came tumbling after

Then up Jack got and home did trot
  As fast as he could caper
And went to bed and patched his head
  With vinegar and brown paper

GOING BROWN

I'm not going to pieces and I'm not going to ground
And I'm not going crazy and I'm not going round
And I'm not going to seed and I'm not going to touch
And I'm not going halves and I'm not going Dutch
And I'm not going up and I'm not going down

—— I'm lying in the sun, going brown

TOFFEE NOSE

Swell, snob, big-wig, nob
Off his lordship goes
Hope he grows a wooden peg
And a toffee nose

BROWN BILL AND BROWN BESS

If you'd been a foot soldier in the 16th Century you'd have gone to war with a Brown Bill – a brown-painted halberd which was something between an extremely heavy axe and a rather blunt spear. Much better, if you had to be a soldier at all, to have been born in the 19th Century. Then you'd have been issued with an absolutely up-to-the-minute flint-lock musket called a Brown Bess after its walnut stock. No doubt you'd have found her a touch more wieldy about the battle field than the old Brown Bill.

GONE PUCE

The Latin for a flea was *pulex* and the French for a flea is *puce*. If you could see one, under a microscope perhaps, a flea is purplish-brown. So if someone says, *You've gone puce*, it means you've gone far worse than red. You've gone flea-coloured or purplish-brown.

MAUVE MONSTERS

Round the town, when I was young, old ladies went in droves
  Their hair was coloured curiously, a sea of different mauves
I hid behind my mother's back while finding ways to peep
  Deciding they were monsters who'd come shopping from the deep
And still a little chilled and thrilled, I wonder to this day
  Why no one thought to tell them we'd have MUCH preferred them grey

SUGARED VIOLETS

Perched like tiny butterflies
  Under a clear glass dome
The sweetly scented violets lay
  And thought, no doubt, of home
For captured now and crystallised
  And far from woodland streams
These sweetly sugared violets
  Were topping chocolate creams

A ROYAL RAGE

He was livid, he was purple, he was heliotrope with rage
  He was Emperor and knew it all too well
Yet he wondered how his subjects and his citizens and serfs
  Would know that he was Emperor or tell

"Bring me robes," he said, "of purple, and the colour of my anger
  For I'm Emperor Celestial on High
And everyone should know it, every citizen and serf
  Every subject passing accidentally by"

So they brought him robes of purple and of heliotrope, magenta
  And they said, "Imperial Highness, you're a wow!"
And immediately his fury and his purple rage subsided
  Now he felt he looked *an Emperor – and how!*

MULBERRY BUSH

Here we go round the mulberry bush
The mulberry bush, the mulberry bush
Here we go round the mulberry bush
  On a cold and frosty morning

LAVENDER IN PURPLE PROSE

Ah, lavender! 'Tis well you grow, in clouds of blue, traced with red to bring us lavender, pure lavender, your own sweet hue. Wild you sprang at first, on dry thankless ground like generous larders for the thirsty bee, then let yourself be tamed, field on field, hazily under the beating sun. And since, how many heated brows and throbbing wrists have your cool waters stilled? Your oils soothed? Between how many linens, cottons, satins, silks have your enduring flowers lain, made fragrant and perfumed? And what of summers past and childhood paths? Though you but brushed them lightly, are they not all lavender-remembered still?

SHRINKING VIOLET

Of all the flowers in the wood
That ornament the ground
The one that peeps most shyly
Is the violet, it's found
As if afraid of being crushed
Ashamed for being small
It seems to half-apologise
For being there at all
And that is why we often say
Of someone that we love
– "Ah yes, a shrinking violet" –
When acting as above.

THE FOXGLOVE AND THE HEATHER

In the highlands, in the heather
  Foxglove raised its head
"I bring gloves for well-dressed foxes
  You just stay in bed."
In the highlands, Heather answered
  Spoke her weathered mind
  "I bring charms, much-needed fortune
Luck to all mankind."

LILAC TIME

Go down to Kew in lilac-time, in lilac-time, in
  lilac-time
Go down to Kew in lilac-time (it isn't far from
  London)
And you shall wander hand in hand with love
  in summer's wonderland;
Go down to Kew in lilac-time (it isn't far from
  London)